George MacDonald

Far above rubies. A novel

George MacDonald

Far above rubies. A novel

ISBN/EAN: 9783741191312

Manufactured in Europe, USA, Canada, Australia, Japa

Cover: Foto ©Andreas Hilbeck / pixelio.de

Manufactured and distributed by brebook publishing software (www.brebook.com)

George MacDonald

Far above rubies. A novel

Far above Rubies.

HECTOR MACINTOSH was a young man about five-and-twenty, who, with the proclivities of the Celt, inherited also some of the consequent disabilities, as well as some that were accidental. Among the rest was a strong tendency to regard only the ideal, and turn away from any authority derived from an inferior source. His chief delight lay in the attempt to embody, in what seemed to him the natural form of verse, the thoughts in him constantly moving at least in the direction of the ideal, even when he was most conscious of his inability to attain to the utterance of them. But it was only in the retirement of his own chamber that he attempted their embodiment; of all things, he shrank from any communion whatever concerning these cherished matters. Nor, indeed, had he any friends who could tempt him to share with them what seemed to him his best; so that, in truth, he was intimate with none. His mind would dwell much upon love and friendship in the imaginary abstract, but of neither had he had the smallest immediate experience. He had cherished only the ideals of the purest and highest sort of either passion, and seemed to find satisfaction enough in the endeavor to embody such in his verse, without even imagining himself in communication with any visionary public. The era had not yet dawned when every scribbler is consumed with the vain ambition of being recognized, not, indeed, as what he is, but as what he pictures himself in his secret sessions of thought. That disease could hardly attack him while yet his very imaginations recoiled from the thought of the inimical presence of a stranger consciousness. Whether this was modesty, or had its hidden base in conceit, I am, with the few insights I have had into his mind, unable to determine.

That he had leisure for the indulgence of his bent was the result of his peculiar position. He lived in the house of his father, and was in his father's employment, so that he was able both to accommodate himself to his father's requirements and at the same time fully indulge his own especial taste. The elder Macintosh was a banker in one of the larger county towns of Scotland—at least, such is the profession and position there accorded by popular consent to one who is, in fact, only a bank-agent, for it is a post involving a good deal of influence and a yet greater responsibility. Of this responsibility, however, he had allowed his son to feel nothing, merely using him as a clerk, and leaving him, as soon as the stated hour for his office-work expired, free in mind as well as body, until the new day should make a fresh claim upon his time and attention. His mother seldom saw him except at meals, and, indeed, although he always behaved dutifully to her, there was literally no intercommunion of thought or feeling between them—a fact which probably had a good deal to do with the undeveloped condition in which Hector found, or rather, did not find himself. Occasionally his mother wanted him to accompany her for a call, but he avoided yielding as much as possible, and generally with success; for this was one of the claims of social convention against which he steadily rebelled—the more determinedly that in none of his mother's friends could he take the smallest interest; for she was essentially a commonplace because ambitious woman, without a spark of aspiration, and her friends were of the same sort, without regard for anything but what was—or, at least, they supposed to be—the fashion. Indeed, it was hard to understand how Hector came ever to be born of such a woman, although in truth she was of as pure Celtic origin as her husband—only blood is not spirit, and that is often clearly manifest. His father, on the other hand, was not without some signs of an imagination—quite undeveloped, indeed, and, I believe, suppressed by the requirements of his business relations. At the same time, Hector knew that he cherished not a little indignation against the insolence of the good Dr. Johnson in regard to both Ossian and his humble translator, Macpherson, upholding the genuineness of both, although unable to enter into and set forth the points of the argument on either side. As to Hector, he reveled in the ancient traditions of his family, and not unfrequently in his earlier youth had made an attempt to re-embody some of its legends into English, vain as regarded the retention of the special airiness and suggestiveness of their vaguely showing symbolism, for often he dropped his pen with a sigh of despair at the illusiveness of the special aroma of the Celtic imagination. For the rest, he had had as good an education as Scotland could in those days afford him, one of whose best features was the negative one that it did not at all interfere with the natural course of his inborn tendencies, and merely developed the power of expressing himself in what manner he might think fit. Let me add that he had a good conscience—I mean, a conscience ready to give him warning of the least tendency to overstep any line of prohibition; and that, as yet, he had never consciously refused to attend to such warning.

Another thing I must mention is that, although his mind was constantly haunted by imaginary forms of loveliness, he had never yet been what is called *in love*. For he had never yet seen anyone who even approached his idea of spiritual at once and physical attraction. He was content to live and wait, without even the notion that he was waiting for anything. He went on writing his verses, and receiving the reward, such as it was, of having placed on record the thoughts which had come to him, so that he might at will recall them. Neither had he any thought of the mental soil which was thus slowly gathering for the possible growth of an unknown seed, fit for growing and developing in that same unknown soil.

One day there arrived in that cold Northern city a certain cold, sunshiny morning, gay and sparkling, and with it the beginning of what, for want of a better word, we may call his fate. He knew nothing of its approach, had not the slightest prevision that the divinity had that moment put his hand to the shaping of his roughhewn ends. It was early October by the calendar, but leaves brown and spotted and dry lay already in little heaps on the pavement—heaps made and unmade continually, as if for the sport of the keen wind that now scattered them with a rush, and again, extemporizing a little evanescent whirlpool, gathered a fresh heap upon the flags, again to rush asunder, as in direst terror of the fresh-invading wind, determined yet again to scatter them, a broken rout of escaping fugitives. Along the pavement, seemingly in furtherance of the careless design of the wind, a girl went heedlessly scushling along among the unresting and unresisting leaves, making with her rather short skirt a mimic whirlwind of her own. Her eyes were fixed on the ground, and she seemed absorbed in anxious thought, which thought had its origin in one of the commonest causes of human perplexity—the need of money, and the impossibility of devising a scheme by which to procure any. It was but a few weeks since her father had died, leaving behind him such a scanty provision for his widow and child that only by the utmost care and coaxing were they able from the first to make it meet their necessities. Nor, indeed, would it have been possible for them to subsist had not a brother of the widow supplemented their poor resources with an uncertain contingent, whose continuance he was not able to secure, or even dared to promise.

At the present moment, however, it was not anxiety as to their own affairs that occupied the mind of Annie Melville, near enough as that might have lain; it was the unhappy condition in which the imprudence of a school-friend—almost her only friend—had involved herself by her hasty marriage with a man who, up to the present moment, had shown no faculty for helping himself or the wife he had involved in his fate, and who did not know where or by what means to procure even the bread of which they were in immediate want.

Now Annie had never had to suffer hunger, and the idea that her companion from childhood should be exposed to such a fate was what she could not bear. Yet, for any way out of it she could see, it would have to be borne. She might possibly, by herself going without, have given her a good piece of bread; but then she would certainly share it with her foolish husband, and there would be little satisfaction in that! They had already arrived at a stage in their downward progress when not gold, or even silver, but bare copper, was lacking as the equivalent for the bread that could but keep them alive until the next rousing of the hunger that even now lay across their threshold. And how could she, in her all but absolute poverty, do anything? Her mother was but one pace or so from the same goal, and would, as a mother must, interfere to prevent her useless postponement of the inevitable. It was clear she could do nothing—and yet she could ill consent that it should be so.

When her father almost suddenly left them alone, Annie was already acting as assistant in the Girls' High School—but, alas! without any recognition of her services by even a promise of coming payment. She lived only in the hope of a small salary, dependent on her definite appointment to the office. To attempt to draw upon this hope would be to imperil the appointment itself. She could not, even for her friend, risk her mother's prospects, already poor enough; and she could not help perceiving the hopelessness of her friend's case, because of the utter characterlessness of the husband to whom she was enslaved. Why interfere with the hunger he would do nothing to forestall? How could she even give such a man the sixpence which had been her father's last gift to her?

But Annie was one to whom, in the course of her life, something strange had not unfrequently happened, chiefly in the shape of what the common mind would set aside as mere coincidence. I do not say *many* such things had occurred in her life; but, together, their strangeness and their recurrence had caused her to remember every one of them, so that, when she reviewed them, they seemed to her many. And now, with a shadowy prevision, as it seemed, that something was going to happen, and with a shadowy recollection that she had known beforehand it was coming, something strange did take place. Of such things she used, in after days, always to employ the old, stately Bible-phrase, "It came to pass"; she never said, "It happened."

As she walked along with her eyes on the ground, the withered leaves caught up every now and then in a wild dance by the frolicsome wind, she was suddenly aware of something among them which she could not identify, whirling in the aërial vortex about her feet. Scarcely caring what it was, she yet, all but mechanically, looked at it a little closer, lost it from sight, caught it again, as a fresh blast sent it once more gyrating about her feet, and now regarded it more steadfastly. Even then it looked like nothing but another withered leaf, brown and wrinkled, given over to the wind, and rustling along at its mercy. Yet it made an impression upon her so far unlike that of a leaf that for a moment more she fixed on it a still keener look of unconsciously expectant eyes, and saw only that it looked—perhaps a little larger than most of the other leaves, but as brown and dead as they. Almost the same instant, however, she turned and pounced upon it, and, the moment she handled it, became aware that it felt less crumbly and brittle than the others looked, and then saw clearly that it was not a leaf, but perhaps a rag, or possibly a piece of soiled and rumpled paper. With a curiosity growing to expectation, and in a moment to wondering recognition, she proceeded to uncrumple it carefully and smooth it out tenderly; nor was the process quite completed when she fell upon her knees on the cold flags, her little cloak flowing wide from the clasp at her neck in a yet wilder puff of the bitter wind; but suddenly remembering that she must not be praying in the sight of men, started again to her feet, and, wrapping her closed hand tight in the scanty border of her cloak, hurried, with the pound-note she had rescued, to the friend whose need was sorer than her own—not without an undefined anxiety in her heart whether she was doing right. How much good the note did, or whether it merely fell into the bottomless gulf of irremediable loss, I cannot tell. Annie's friend and her shiftless mate at once changed their dirty piece of paper for silver, bought food and railway tickets, left the town, and disappeared entirely from her horizon.

But consequences were not over with Annie; and the next day she became acquainted with the fact that proved of great significance to her, namely, that the same evening she found the money, Mr. Mackintosh's kitchen-chimney had been on fire; and it wanted but the knowledge of how this had taken place to change the girl's consciousness from that of one specially aided by the ministry of an angel to that of a young woman, honest hitherto, suddenly changed into a thief!

For, in the course of a certain

FAR ABOVE RUBIES

friendly gossip's narrative, it came out that that night the banker had been using the kitchen fire for the destruction of an accumulation of bank-notes, the common currency of Scotland, which had been judged altogether too dirty, or too much dilapidated, to be reissued. The knowledge of this fact was the slam of the closing door, whereby Annie found her soul shut out to wander in a night of dismay. The woman who told the fact saw nothing of consequence in it; Mrs. Melville, to whom she was telling it, saw nothing but perhaps a lesson on the duty of having chimneys regularly swept, because of the danger to neighboring thatch. But had not Annie been seated in the shadow, her ghastly countenance would, even to the most casual glance, have betrayed a certain guilty horror, for now she *knew* that she had found and given away what she ought at once to have handed back to its rightful owner. It was true he did not even know that he had lost it, and could have no suspicion that she had found it; but what difference did or could that make? It was true also that she had neither taken nor bestowed it to her own advantage; but again, what difference could that make in her duty to restore it? Did she not well remember how eloquently and precisely Mr. Kennedy had, the very last Sunday, expounded the passage, " Thou shalt not respect the person of the poor." Right was right, whatever soft-hearted people might say or think. Anyone might give what was his own, but who could be right in giving away what was another's? It was true she had done it without thinking; but she had known, or might have known, well enough that to whomsoever it might belong, it was not hers. And now what possibility was there of setting right what she had set wrong? It was just possible a day might come when she should be able to restore what she had unjustly taken, but at the present moment it was as impossible for her to lay her hand upon a pound-note as upon a million. And, terrible thought!—she might have to enter the presence of her father—dead, men called him, but alive she knew him—with the consciousness that she had not brought him back the honor he had left with her.

It will, of course, suggest itself to every reader that herein she was driving her sense of obligation to the verge of foolishness; and, indeed, the thought did not fail to occur even to herself; but the answer of the self-accusing spirit was that had she been thoroughly upright in heart, she would at once have gone to the nearest house and made such inquiry as must instantly have resulted in the discovery of what had happened. This she had omitted—without thought, it is true, but not, therefore, without blame; and now, so far as she could tell, she would never be able to make restitution! Had she even told her mother what befallen her,

her mother might have thought of the way in which it had come to pass, and set her feet in the path of her duty! But she had made evil haste, and had compassed too much.

She found herself, in truth, in a sore predicament, and was on the point of starting to her feet to run and confess to Mr. Macintosh what she had done, that he might at once pronounce the penalty on what she never doubted he must regard as a case of simple theft; but she bethought herself that she would remain incapable of offering the least satisfaction, and must therefore be regarded merely as one who sought by confession to secure forgiveness and remission. What proof had she to offer even that she had given the money away? To mention the name of her friend would be to bring her into discredit, and transfer to her the blame of her own act. There was nothing she could do—and yet, however was she to go about with such a load upon her conscience? Confessing, she might at least be regarded as one who desired and meant to be honest. Confession would, anyhow, ease the weight of her load. Passively at last, from very weariness of thought, her mind was but going backward and forward over its own traces, heedlessly obliterating them, when suddenly a new and horrid consciousness emerged from the trodden slime—that she was glad that at least Sophy *had* the money! For one passing moment she was glad with the joy of Lady

Macbeth, that what was done was done, and could not be altered. Then once more the storm within her awoke and would not again be stilled.

But now a third something happened which brought with it hope, for it suggested a way of deliverance. Impelled by the same power that causes a murderer to haunt the scene of his violence, she left the house, and was unaware whither she was directing her steps until she found herself again passing the door of the banker's house; there, in that same kitchen-window, on a level with the pavement, she espied, in large pen-drawn print, the production apparently of the cook or another of the servants, the announcement that a parlor-maid was wanted immediately. Again without waiting to think, and only afterwards waking up to the fact and meaning of what she had done, she turned, went back to the entry-door, and knocked. It was almost suddenly opened by the cook, and at once the storm of her misery was assuaged in a rising moon of hope, and the night became light about her. Ah, through what miseries are not even frail hopes our best and safest, our only *true* guides indeed, into other and yet fairer hopes!

"Did you want to see the mistress?" asked the jolly-faced cook, where she stood on the other side of the threshold; and, without waiting an answer, she turned and led the way to the parlor. Annie followed, as if across the foundation of the fallen wall of Jericho; and found, to her surprise, that Mrs. Macintosh, knowing her by sight, received her with condescension, and Annie, grateful for the good-humor which she took for kindness, told her simply that she had come to see whether she would accept her services as parlor-maid.

Mrs. Macintosh seemed surprised at the proposal, and asked her the natural question whether she had ever occupied a similar situation.

Annie answered she had not, but that at home, while her father was alive, she had done so much of the same sort that she believed she could speedily learn all that was necessary.

"I thought someone told me," said the lady, who was one of the greatest gossips in the town, "that you were one of the teachers in the High School?"

"That is true," answered Annie; "I was doing so upon probation; but I had not yet begun to receive any salary for it. I was only a sort of apprentice to the work, and under no engagement."

Mrs. Macintosh, after regarding Annie for some time, and taking silent observation of her modesty and good-breeding, said at last:

"I like the look of you, Miss——, Miss——"

"My name is Annie Melville."

"Well, Annie, I confess I do not indeed *see* anything particularly unsuitable in you, but at the same time I cannot help fearing you may be—or, I should say rather, may imagine yourself—superior to what may be required of you."

"Oh, no, ma'am!" answered Annie; "I assure you I am too poor to think of any such thing! Indeed, I am so anxious to make money at once that, if you would consent to give me a trial, I should be ready to come to you this very evening."

"You will have no wages before the end of your six months."

"I understand, ma'am."

"It is a risk to take you without a character."

"I am very sorry, ma'am; but I have no one that can vouch for me—except, indeed, Mrs. Slater, of the High School, would say a word in my favor."

"Well, well!" answered Mrs. Macintosh, "I am so far pleased with you that I do not think I can be making a *great* mistake if I merely give you a trial. You may come to-night, if you like—that is, with your mother's permission."

Annie ran home greatly relieved, and told her mother what a piece of good-fortune she had had. Mrs. Melville did not at all take to the idea at first, for she cherished undefined expections for Annie, and knew that her father had done so also, for the girl was always reading, and had been for years in the habit of reading aloud to him, making now and then a remark that showed she understood well what she read. So the mother took comfort in her disappointment that her child had, solely for her sake, she supposed, betaken herself to such service as would at once secure her livelihood and bring her in a little money, for, with the shadow of coming want growing black above them, even her first half-year's wages was a point of hope and expectation.

"Well, Annie," she answered, after a few moments' consideration, "it is but for a time; and you will be able to give up the place as soon as you please, and the easier that she only takes you on trial; that will hold for you as well as for her."

But nothing was farther from Annie's intention than finding the place would not suit her: no change could she dream of before at least she had a pound-note in her hand, when at once she would make it clear to her mother what a terrible scare had driven her to the sudden step she had taken. Until then she must go about with her whole head sick and her whole heart faint; neither could she for many weeks rid herself of the haunting notion that the banker, who was chiefly affected by her crime,—for as such she fully believed and regarded her deed,—was fully aware of her guilt. It seemed to her, when at any moment he happened to look at her, that now at last he must be on the point of letting her know that he had read the truth in her guilty looks, and she constantly fancied him saying to himself, "That is the girl who stole my money; she feels my eyes upon her." Every time she came home from an errand she would imagine her master looking from the window of his private room on the first floor, in readiness to cast aside forbearance and denounce her: he was only waiting to make himself one shade surer! Ah, how long was the time she had to await her cleansing, the moment when she could go to him and say, "I have wronged, I have robbed you; here is all I can do to show my repentance. All this time I have been but waiting for my wages, to repay what I had taken from you." And, oddly enough, she was always mixing herself up with the man in the parable, who had received from his master a pound to trade with and make more;

from her dreams she would wake in terror at the sound of that master's voice, ordering the pound to be taken from her and given to the schoolfellow whom, at the cost of her own honesty, she had befriended. Oh, joyous day when the doom should be lifted from her, and she set free, to dream no more! For surely, when at length her master knew all, with the depth of her sorrow and repentance, he could not refuse his forgiveness! Would he not even, she dared to hope, remit the interest due on his money?—of which she entertained, in her ignorance, a usurious and preposterous idea.

The days went on, and the hour of her deliverance drew nigh. But, long before it came, two other processes had been slowly arriving at maturity. She had been gaining the confidence of her mistress, so that, ere three months were over, the arrangement of all minor matters of housekeeping was entirely in her hands. It may be that Mrs. Macintosh was not a little lazy, nor sorry to leave aside whatever did not positively demand her personal attention; one thing I am sure of, that Annie never made the smallest attempt to gain this favor, if such it was. Her mistress would, for instance, keep losing the keys of the cellaret, until in despair she at last yielded them entirely to the care of Annie, who thereafter carried them in her pocket, where they were always at hand when wanted.

The other result was equally natural, but of greater importance; Hector, the only child of the house, was gradually and, for a long time, unconsciously falling in love with Annie. Those friends of the family who liked Annie, and felt the charm of her manners and simplicity, said only that his mother had herself to blame, for what else could she expect? Others of them, regarding her from the same point of view as her mistress, repudiated the notion as absurd, saying Hector was not the man to degrade himself! He was incapable of such a misalliance.

But, as I have said already, Hector, although he had never yet been in love, was yet more than usually ready to fall in love, as belongs to the poetic temperament, when the fit person should appear. As to what sort she might prove depended on two facts in Hector—one, that he was fastidious in the best meaning of the word, and the other that he was dominated by sound good sense; a fact which even his father allowed, although with a grudge, seeing he had hitherto manifested no devotion to business, but spent his free time in literary pursuits. Of the special nature of those pursuits his father knew, or cared to know, nothing; and as to his mother, she had not even a favorite hymn.

I may say, then, that the love of womankind, which in solution, so to speak, pervaded every atomic interstice of the nature of Hector, had gradually, indeed, but yet rapidly, concentrated and crystallized around the idea of Annie—the more homogeneously and absorbingly that she was the first who had so moved him. It was, indeed, in the case of each a first love, although in the case of neither love at first sight.

Almost from the hour when first Annie entered the family, Hector had looked on her with eyes of interest; but, for a time, she had gone about the house with a sense almost of being there upon false pretenses, for she knew that she was doing what she did from no regard to any of its members, but only to gain the money whose payment would relieve her from an ever-present consciousness of guilt; and for this cause, if for no other, she was not in danger of falling in love with Hector. She was, indeed, too full of veneration for her master and mistress, and for their son so immeasurably above her, to let her thoughts rest upon him in any but a distantly worshipful fashion.

But it was part of her duty, which was not over well-defined in the house, to see that her young master's room was kept tidy and properly dusted; and in attending to this it was unavoidable that she should come upon indications of the way in which he spent his leisure hours. Never dreaming, indeed, that a servant might recognize at a glance what his father and mother did not care to know, Hector was never at any pains to conceal, or even to lay aside the lines yet wet from his pen when he left the room; and Annie could not help seeing them, or knowing what they were. Like many another Scotch lassie, she was fonder of reading than of anything else; and in her father's house she had had the free use of what books were in it; nor is it, then, to be wondered at that she was far more familiar with certain great books than was ever many an Oxford man. Some never read what they have no desire to assimilate; and some read what no expenditure of reading could ever make them able to appropriate; but Annie read, understood, and re-read the " Paradise Lost"; knew intimately " Comus" as well; delighted in " Lycidas," and had some of Milton's sonnets by heart; while for the Hymn on the Nativity, she knew every line, had studied every turn and phrase in it. It is sometimes a great advantage not to have many books, and so never outgrow the sense of mystery that hovers about even an open book-case; it was with awe and reverence that Annie, looking around Hector's room, saw in it, not daring to touch them, books she had heard of, but never seen—among others a Shakspere in one thick volume lay open on his table; nor is it, then, surprising that, when putting his papers straight, she could not help seeing from the different lengths of the lines upon them that they were verse. She trembled and glowed at the very sight of them, for she had in herself the instinct of sacred numbers, and in her soul felt a vague hunger after what might be contained in those loose papers—into which she did not even peep, instinctively knowing it dishonorable. She trembled yet more at recognizing the beautiful youth in the same house with her, to whom she did service, as himself one of those gifted creatures whom most she revered—a poet, perhaps another such as Milton! Neither are all ladies, nor all servants of ladies, honorable like Annie, or fit as she to be left alone with a man's papers.

Hector knew very well how his mother would regard such an alliance as had now begun to absorb every desire and thought of his heart, and was the more careful to watch and repress every sign of the same, foreseeing that, at the least suspicion of the fact, she would lay all the blame upon Annie, at once dismiss her from the house, and remain forever convinced that she had entered it with the design in her heart to make him fall in love with her. He therefore avoided ever addressing her, except with a distant civility, the easier to him that his mind was known only to himself, while all the time the consciousness of her presence in it enveloped the house in a rosy cloud. For a long time he did not even dream of attempting a word with her alone, fondly imagining that thus he gave his mother time to know and love Annie before discovering anything between them to which she might object. But he did not yet know how incapable that mother was of any simple affection, being, indeed, one of the commonest-minded of women. He believed also that the least attempt to attract Annie's attention would but scare her, and make her incapable of listening to what he might try to say.

In the meantime, Annie, under the influence of more and better food, and that freedom from care which came of the consciousness that she was doing her best both for her mother and for her own moral emancipation, looked sweeter and grew happier every day; no cloudy sense, no doubt of approaching danger had yet begun to heave an ugly shoulder above her horizon, neither had Hector begun to fret against the feeling that he must not speak to her; in such a silence and in such a presence he felt he could live happy for ages; he moved in a lovely dream of still content.

And it was natural also that he should begin to burgeon spiritually and mentally, to grow and flourish beyond any experience in the past. Within a few such days of hidden happiness, the power of verse, and of thoughts worthy of verse, came upon him with as sure an inspiration of the Almighty as can ever descend upon a man, accompanied by a deeper sense of the being and the presence of God, and a stronger desire to do the will of the Father, which is surely the best thing God himself can kindle in the heart of any man. For what good is there in creation but the possibility of being yet further created? And what else is growth but more of the will of God?

Something fresh began to stir in his mind; even as in the spring, away in far depths of beginning, the sap gives its first upward throb in the tree, and the first bud, as yet invisible, begins to jerk itself forward to break from the cerements of ante-natal quiescence, and become a growing leaf, so a something in Hector that was his very life and soul began to yield to unseen creative impulse, and throb with a dim, divine consciousness. The second evening after thus recognizing its presence he hurried up the stair from the office to his own room, and there, sitting down, began to write—not a sonnet to his charmer, neither any dream about her, not even some sweet song of the waking spring which he felt moving within him, but the first speech of a dramatic poem, It was a bold beginning, but all beginners are daring, if not presumptuous. Hector's aim was to embody an ideal of check, of rousing, of revival, of new energy and fresh start. All that evening he wrote with running pen, forgot the dinner-bell after its first summons, and went on until Annie knocked at his door, dispatched to summon him to the meal. There was in Hector, indeed, as a small part of the world came by-and-by to know, the making of a real poet, for such there are in the world at all times—yea, even now—although they may not be recognized, or even intended to ripen in the course of one human season. I think Annie herself was one of such—so full was she of receptive and responsive faculty in the same kind, and I remain in doubt whether the genuine enjoyment of verse be not a fuller sign of the presence of what is most valuable in it than even some power of producing it. For Hector, I imagine, it gave strong proof of his being a poet indeed that, when he opened the door to her knock, the appearance of Annie herself, instead of giving him a thrill of pleasure, occasioned him a little annoyance by the evanishment of a just culminating train of thought into the vast and seething void, into which he gazed after it in vain. And Annie herself, although all the time in Hector's thought, revealed herself only, after the custom of celestials, at the very moment of her disappearance; her message delivered, she went back to her duties at the table; and then first Hector woke to the knowledge that she had been at his door, and was there no more. During the last few days he had been gradually approaching the resolve to keep silence no longer, but be bold and tell Annie how full his heart was of her. One moment he might have done so; one moment more, and he could not!

He followed close upon her steps, but not a word with her was possible, and it seemed to Hector that she sped from him like a very wraith to avoid his addressing her. Had she, then, he asked himself, some dim suspicion of his feelings toward her, or was she but making haste from a sense of propriety?

Now that very morning Mrs. Macintosh had been talking kindly to Annie—as kindly, that is, as her abominable condescension would permit—and, what to Annie was of far greater consequence, had paid her her wages, rather more than she had expected, so that nothing now lay between her and the fall of her burden from her heavy-laden conscience, except, indeed, her preliminary confession. Dinner, therefore, being over, her mistress gone to the drawing room to prepare the coffee, and her master to his room to write a letter suddenly remembered,

Hector was left alone with Annie. Whereupon followed an amusing succession of disconnected attempt and frustration. For no sooner had Mr. Macintosh left the room than Annie darted from it after him, and Hector darted after Annie, determined at length to speak to her. When Annie, however, reached the foot of the stair, her master was already up the first flight, and Annie's courage failing her, she, turning sharply round, almost ran against Hector, who was close behind her. The look of disappointment on her face, to the meaning of which he had no clew, quenching his courage next, he returned in silence to the dining room, where Annie was now hovering aimlessly about the table, until, upon his re-entrance, she settled herself behind Hector's chair. He turned half-round, and would have said something to her; but, seeing her pale and troubled, he lapsed into a fit of brooding, and no longer dared speak to her. Besides, his mother might come to the dining room at any moment!

Then Annie, thinking she heard her master's re-descending step, hurried again from the room; but only at once to return afresh, which set Hector wondering yet more. Why on earth should she be lying in ambush for his father? He did not know that she was equally anxious to avoid the eyes of her mistress. And while Annie was anxious to keep her secret from the tongue of Mrs. Macintosh, Hector was as anxious to keep his from the eyes of his mother until a fit moment should arrive for its disclosure. But he imagined, I believe, that Annie saw he wanted to speak to her, and thought she was doing what she could to balk his intention.

But the necessity for disclosure was strongest in Annie, and drove her to encounter what risk might be involved. So when at last she heard a certain step of the stair creak, she darted to the door, and left the room even while the hand of her mistress, coming to say the coffee was ready, was on that which communciated with the drawing room.

"I thought I heard Annie at the sideboard: is she gone?" she said.

"She left the room this moment, I believe," answered Hector.

"What is she gone for?"

"I cannot say, mother," replied Hector indifferently, in the act himself of leaving the room also, determined on yet another attempt to speak to Annie.

In the meantime, however, Annie had found her opportunity. She had met Mr. Macintosh halfway down the last flight of stairs, and had lifted to him such a face of entreaty that he listened at once to her prayer for a private interview, and, turning, led the way up again to the room he had just left. There he shut the door, and said to her pleasantly:

"Well, Annie, what is it?"

I am afraid his man-imagination had led him to anticipate some complaint against Hector: he certainly was nowise prepared for what the poor self-accusing girl had to say.

For one moment she stood unable to begin; the next she had recovered her resolution: her face filled with a sudden glow; and ere her master had time to feel shocked, she was on her knees at his feet, holding up to him a new pound-note, one of those her mistress had just given her. Familiar, however, as her master was with the mean-looking things in which lay almost all his dealings, he did not at first recognize the object she offered him; while what connection with his wife's parlor-maid it could represent was naturally inconceivable to him. He stood for a moment staring at the note, and then dropped a pair of dull, questioning eyes on the face of the kneeling girl. He was not a man of quick apprehension, and the situation was appallingly void of helpful suggestion. To make things yet more perplexing, Annie sobbed as if her heart would break, and was unable to utter a word. "What must a stranger imagine," the poor man thought, "to come upon such a tableau?" Her irrepressible emotion lasted so long that he lost his patience and turned upon her, saying:

"I must call your mistress; she will know what to do with you!" Instantly she sprang to her feet, and broke into passionate entreaty.

"Oh, please, *please*, sir, have a minute's patience with me," she cried; "you never saw me behave so badly before!"

"Certainly not, Annie; I never did. And I hope you will never do so again," answered her master, with reviving good-nature, and was back in his first notion, that Hector had said something to her which she thought rude and did not like to repeat. He had never had a daughter, and perhaps all the more felt pitiful over the troubled woman-child at his feet.

But, having once spoken out and conquered the spell upon her, Annie was able to go on. She became suddenly quiet, and, interrupted only by an occasional sob, poured out her whole story, if not quite unbrokenly, at least without actual intermission, while her master stood and listened without a break in his fixed attention. By-and-by, however, a slow smile began to dawn on his countenance, which spread and spread until at length he burst into a laugh, none the less merry that it was low and evidently restrained lest it should be overheard. Like one suddenly made ashamed, Annie rose to her feet, but still held out the note to her master.

How was it possible that her evil deed should provoke her master to a fit of laughter? It might be easy for him in his goodness to pardon her, but how could he treat her offense as a thing of no consequence? Was it not a sin, which, like every other sin, could nowise at all be cleansed? For even God himself could not blot out the fact that she had done the deed! And yet, there stood her master laughing! And, what was more dreadful still, despite the resentment of her conscience, her master's merriment so far affected herself that she could not repress a responsive smile! It was no less than indecent, and yet, even in that answering smile, her misery of six months' duration passed totally away, melted from her like a mist of the morning, so that she could not even recall the feeling of her lost unhappiness. But, might not her conscience be going to sleep? Was it not possible she might be growing indifferent to right and wrong? Was she not aware in herself that there were powers of evil about her, seeking to lead her astray, and putting strange and horrid things in her mind?

But, although he laughed, her

master uttered no articulate sound until she had ended her statement, by which time his amusement had changed to admiration. Another minute still passed, however, before he knew what answer to make.

"But, my good girl," he began, "I do not see that you have anything to blame yourself for—at least, not anything *worth* blaming yourself about. After so long a time, the money found was certainly your own, and you could do what you pleased with it."

"But, sir, I did not wait at all to see how it had happened, or whether it might not be claimed. I believe, indeed, that I hurried away at once, lest anyone should know I had it. I ran to spend it at once, so for whatever happened afterward I was to blame. Then, when it was too late, I learned that the money was yours!"

"What did you do with it, if I may ask?" said the master.

"I gave it to a schoolfellow of mine who had married a helpless sort of husband and was in want of food."

"I am afraid you did not help them much by that," murmured the banker.

"Please, sir, I knew no other way to help them; and the money seemed to have been given me for them. I soon came to know better, and have been sorry ever since. I knew that I had no right to give it away as soon as I knew whose it was."

She ceased, but still held out the note to him.

Mr. Macintosh stood again silent, and made no movement toward taking it.

"Please, sir, take the money, and forgive me," pleaded Annie. "And please, sir, *please* do not say anything about it to anybody. Even my mother does not know."

"Now there you did wrong. You ought to have told your mother."

"I see that now, sir; but I was so glad to be able to help the poor creatures that I did not think of it till afterwards."

"I dare say your mother would have been glad of the money herself; I understand she was not left very well off."

"At that time I did not know she was so poor. But now that my mistress has paid me such good wages, I am going to take her every penny of them this very afternoon."

"And then you will tell her, will you not?"

"I shall not mind telling her when you have taken it back. I was afraid to tell her before! It was to pay you back that I asked Mrs. Macintosh to take me for parlor-maid."

"Then you were not in service before?"

"No, sir. You see, my mother thought I could earn my bread in a way we should both like better."

"So now you will give up service and go back to her?"

"I am not sure, sir. It would be long, I fear, before the school would pay me as well. You see, I have my food here too. And everything tells. Please, sir, take the pound."

"My dear girl," said her master, "I could not think of depriving you of what you have so well earned. It is more than enough to me that you want to repay it. I positively cannot take it."

"Indeed, I do want to repay it, sir," rejoined Annie. "It's anything but willing I shall be *not* to repay it. Indeed, there is no other way to get my soul free."

Here it seems time I should mention that Hector, weary of waiting Annie's return, had left the dining room to look for her; and running up the stair, not without the dread of hearing his mother's foot behind him, had slid softly into his father's room, to find Annie on her knees before him, and hear enough to understand her story before either his father or she was aware of his presence.

"I beg your pardon, sir, but indeed you must take it," urged Annie. "Surely you would not be so cruel to a poor girl who prays you to take the guilt off her back. Don't you see, sir, I never can look my father in the face till I have paid the money back!"

Here his father caught sight of Hector, and, perceiving that Annie had not yet seen him, and possibly glad of a witness, put up his hand to him to keep still.

"Where is your father, then?" he asked Annie.

"In heaven somewhere," she answered, "waiting for my mother and me. Oh, father!" she broke out, "if only you had been alive you would soon have got me out of my shame and misery! But, thank God! it will soon be over now; my master cannot refuse to set me free."

"Certainly I will set you free," said Mr. Macintosh, a good deal touched. "With all my heart I forgive you the—the—the debt, and I thank you for bringing me to know the honestest girl—I mean, the most honorable girl I have ever yet had the pleasure to meet."

Hector had been listening, hardly able to contain his delight, and at these last words of his father, like the blundering idiot he was, he rushed forward, and, clasping Annie to his heart, cried out:

"Thank God, Annie, my father at least knows what you are!"

He met with a rough and astounding check. Far too startled to see who it was that thus embraced her, and unprepared to receive such a salutation, least of all from one she had hitherto regarded as the very prince of gentleness and courtesy, she met it with a sound, ringing box on the ear, which literally staggered Hector, and sent his father into a second peal of laughter, this time as loud as it was merry, and the next moment swelled in volume by that of Hector himself.

"Thank you, Annie!" he cried. "I never should have thought you could hit so hard. But, indeed, I beg your pardon. I forgot myself and you too when I behaved so badly. But I'm not sorry, father, after all, for that box on the ear has got me over a difficult task, and compelled me to speak out at once what has been long in my mind, but which I had not the courage to say. Annie," he went on, turning to her, and standing humbly before her, "I have long loved you; if you will do me the honor to marry me, I am yours the moment you say so."

But Annie's surprise and the hasty act she had committed in the first impulse of defense had so reacted upon her in a white dismay that she stood before him speechless and almost ready to drop. Awakening from what was fast growing a mere dream of offense to the assured consciousness of another offense almost as flagrant, she stared as if she had suddenly opened her eyes on a whole Walpurgisnacht of demons and witches, while Hector, recovering from his astonishment to the lively delight of having something to pretend at least to forgive Annie, and yielding to sudden Celtic impulse, knelt at her feet, seized her hand, which she had no power to withdraw from him, covered it with eager kisses and placed it on his head. Little more would have made him cast himself prone before her, lift her foot, and place it on his neck.

But his father brought a little of his common sense to the rescue.

"Tut, Hector!" he said; "give the lass time to come to her senses. Would you woo her like a raving maniac? I don't, indeed, wonder, after what you heard her tell me, that you should have taken such a sudden fancy to her; but——"

"Father," interrupted Hector, "it is no fancy—least of all a sudden one! I fell in love with Annie the very first time I saw her waiting at table. It is true I did not understand what had befallen me for some time; but I do, and I did from the first, and now forever I shall both love and worship Annie!"

"Mr. Hector," said Annie, "it was too bad of you to listen. I did not know anyone was there but your father. You were never intended to hear; and I did not think you would have done such a dishonorable thing. It was not like you, Mr. Hector!"

"How was I to know you had

secrets with my father, Annie? Dishonorable or not, the thing is done, and I am glad of it—especially to have heard what you had no intention of telling me."

"I could not have believed it of you, Mr. Hector!" persisted Annie.

"But, now that I think of it," suggested Mr. Macintosh, "may not your mother think she has something to say in the matter between you?"

This was a thought already dawning upon her that terrified Annie; she knew, indeed, perfectly how his mother would regard Hector's proposal, and she dared not refer the matter to her decision.

"I must be out of the house first, Mr. Hector," she said—and I think she meant—"before I confess my love."

The impression Annie had made upon her master may be judged from the fact that he rose and went, leaving his son and the parlor-maid together.

What then passed between them I cannot narrate precisely. Overwhelmed by Hector's avowal, and quite unprepared as she had been for it, it was yet no unwelcome news to Annie. Indeed, the moment he addressed her, she knew in her heart that she had been loving him for a long time, though never acknowledging to herself the fact. Such must often be the case between two whom God has made for each other. And although he were a bold man who said that marriages were made in heaven, he were a bolder who denied that love at first sight was never there decreed. For where God has fitted persons for each other, what can they do but fall mutually in love? Who will then dare to say he did not decree that result? As to what may follow after from their own behavior, I would be as far from saying that was *not* decreed as from saying the conduct itself *was* decreed. Surely there shall be room left, even in the counsels of God, for as much liberty as belongs to our being made in his image—free like him to choose the good and refuse the evil! He who *has* chosen the good remains in the law of liberty, free to choose right again. He who always chooses the right, will at length be free to choose like

God himself, for then shall his will itself be free. Freedom to choose and freedom of the will are two different conditions.

Before the lovers, which it wanted no moment to make them, left the room, they had agreed that Annie must at once leave the house. Hector took her to her mother's door, and when he returned he found that his father and mother had retired. But it may be well that I should tell a little more of what had passed between the lovers before they parted.

Annie's first thought when they were left together was, "Alas! what will my mistress say? She must think the worst possible of me!"

"Oh, Hector!" she broke out,

"whatever will your mother think of me?"

"No good, I'm afraid," answered Hector honestly. "But that is hardly what we have to think of at this precise moment."

"Take back what you said!" cried Annie; "I will promise you never to think of it again—at least, I will *try* never once to do so. It must have been all my fault—though I do not know how, and never dreamed it was coming. Perhaps I shall find out, when I think over it, where I was to blame."

"I have no doubt you are capable of inventing a hundred reasons—after hearing your awful guilty confession to my father, you little innocent!" answered Hector.

And the ice thus broken, things went on a good deal better, and they came to talk freely.

"Of course," said Hector, "I am not so silly or so wicked as to try to persuade you that my mother will open her arms to you. She knows neither you nor herself."

"Will she be terribly angry?" said Annie, with a foreboding quaver in her voice.

"Rather, I am afraid," allowed Hector.

"Then don't you think we had better give it up at once?"

"Never forever!" cried Hector. "That is not what I fell in love with you for! I will not give you up even for Death himself! He is not the ruler of our world. No lover is worthy of the name who does not defy Death and all his works!"

"I am not afraid of him, Hector. I, too, am ready to defy him. But is it right to defy your mother?"

"It is, when she wants one to be false and dishonorable. For herself, I will try to honor her as much as she leaves possible to me. But my mother is not my parents."

"Oh, please, Hector, don't quibble. You would make me doubt you!"

"Well, we won't argue about it. Let us wait to hear what *your* mother will say to it to-morrow, when I come to see you."

"You really will come? How pleased my mother will be!"

"Why, what else should I do? I thought you were just talking of the honor we owe to our parents! Your mother is mine too."

"I was thinking of yours then."

"Well, I dare say I shall have a talk with *my* mother first, but what *your* mother will think is of far more consequence to me. I know only too well what my mother will say; but you must not take that too much to heart. She has always had some girl or other in her mind for me; but if a man has any rights, surely the strongest of all is the right to choose for himself the girl to marry—if she will let him."

"Perhaps his mother would choose better."

"Perhaps you do not know, Annie, that I am five-and-twenty years of age: if I have no right yet to judge for myself, pray when do you suppose I shall?"

"It's not the right I'm thinking of, but the experience."

"Ah, I see! You want me to fall in love with a score of women first, so that I may have a chance of choosing. Really, Annie, I had not thought you would count that a great advantage. For my part, I have never once been in love but with you, and I confess to a fancy that that might almost prove a recommendation to you. But I suppose you will at least allow it desirable that a man should love the girl he marries? If my preference for you be a mere boyish fancy, as probably my mother is at this moment trying to persuade my father, at what age do you suppose it will please

God to give me the heart of a man? My mother is sure to prefer somebody not fit to stand in your dingiest cotton frock. Anybody but you for my wife is a thing unthinkable. God would never degrade me to any choice of my mother's! He knows you for the very best woman I shall ever have the chance of marrying. Shall I tell you the sort of woman my mother would like me to marry? Oh, I know the sort! First, she must be tall and handsome, with red, fashionable hair, and cool, offhand manners. She must never look shy or put out, or as if she did not know what to say. On the contrary, she must know who's who, and what's what, and never wear a dowdy bonnet, but always a stunning hat. And she must have a father who can give her something handsome when she is married. That's my mother's girl for me. I can't bear to look such a girl in the face! She makes me ashamed of myself and of her. The sort I want is one that grows prettier and prettier the more you love and trust her, and always looks best when she is busiest doing something for somebody. Yes, she has black hair, black as the night; and you see the whiteness of her face in the darkest night. And her eyes, they are blue, oh, as blue as bits of the very sky at midnight! and they shine and flash so—just like yours, and nobody else's, my darling."

But here they heard footsteps on the stair—those of Mrs. Macintosh, hurrying up to surprise them. They guessed that her husband had just left her, and that she was in a wild fury; simultaneously they rose and fled. Hector would have led the way quietly out by the front door; but Annie turning the other way to pass through the kitchen, Hector at once turned and followed her. But he had hardly got up with her before she was safe in her mother's house, and the door shut behind them. There Hector bade her goodnight, and, hastening home, found all the lights out, and heard his father and mother talking in their own room; but what they said he never knew.

The next morning Annie had hardly done dressing when she heard a knock at the street-door.

"That'll be Hector, mother," she said. "I'm thinking he'll be come to have a word with you."

"Annie!" exclaimed her mother, in rebuke of the liberty she took. "But if you mean young Mr. Macintosh, what on earth can he want with me?"

"Bide a minute, mother," answered Annie, "and he'll tell you himself."

So Mrs. Melville went to the door and opened it to the young man, who stood there shy and expectant.

"Mrs. Melville," he said, "I have come to tell you that I love your Annie, and want to make her *my* Annie as well. I am more sorry than I can tell you to confess that I am not able to marry at once, but please wait a little while for me. I shall do my best to take you both home with me as soon as possible."

She looked for a moment silently in his face, then, throwing her arms round his neck, answered:

"And I wonder who wouldn't be glad to wait for your sweet face to the very Day of Judgment, sir, when all must have their own at last."

Therewith she burst into tears, and, turning, led the way to the parlor.

"Here's your Hector, Annie," she said as she opened the door. "Take him, and make much of him, for I'm sure he deserves it."

Then she drew him hastily into the room, and closed the door.

"You see," Hector went on, " I must let you both know that my mother is dead against my having Annie. She thinks, of course, that I might do better; but I know she is only far too good for me, and that I shall be a fortunate as well as happy man the day we come together. She has already proved herself as true a woman as ever God made."

"She is that, sir, as I know and can testify, who have known her longer than anybody else. But sit you down and love each other, and never mind me; I'll not be a burden to you as long as I can lift a hand to earn my own bread. And when I'm old and past work, I'll not be too proud to take whatever you can spare me, and eat it with thankfulness."

So they sat down, and were soon making merry together.

But nothing could reconcile Mrs. Macintosh to the thought of Annie for her daughter-in-law; her pride, indignation, and disappointment were much too great, and they showed themselves the worse that her husband would not say a word against either Annie or Hector, who, he insisted, had behaved very well. He would not go a step beyond confessing that the thing was not altogether as he could have wished, but upheld that it contained ground for satisfaction. In vain he called to his wife's mind the fact that neither she nor he were by birth or early position so immeasurably above Annie. Nothing was of any use to calm her; nothing would persuade her that Annie had not sought their service with the express purpose of carrying away her son. Her behavior proved, indeed, that Annie had done prudently in going at once home to her mother, where presently her late mistress sought and found her; acting royally the part of one righteously outraged in her dearest dignity. Her worst enemy could have desired for her nothing more degrading than to see and hear her. She insisted that Hector should abjure Annie, or leave the house. Hector laid the matter before his father. He encouraged him to humor his mother as much as he could, and linger on, not going every night to see the girl, in the hope that time might work some change. But the time passed in bitter reproaches on the part of the mother, and expostulations on the part of the son, and there appeared no sign of the amelioration the father had hoped for. The fact was that Mrs. Macintosh's natural vulgarity had been so pampered by what she regarded as wealth, and she had grown so puffed up, that her very person seemed to hold the door wide for the devil. For self-importance is perhaps a yet deeper root of all evil than even the love of money. Any deep, honest affection might have made it too hot for the devil, but in her heart there was little room for such a love. She seemed to believe in nothing but mode and fashion, to care for nothing but what she called "the thing." She grew in self-bulk, and gathered more and more weight in her own esteem: she wore yet showier and more vulgar clothes, and actually cultivated a slang that soon bade farewell to delicacy, so that she sank and she sank, and she ate and she drank, until at last she impressed her good-natured clergyman himself as one but a very little above the beasts that perish—if, indeed, she was in any respect equal to a good, conscientious dog! She retained, however, this much respect for her son, for which that son gave her little thanks, that by-and-by she limited herself to expending all her contempt upon Annie, and toward Hector settled into a dogged silence, whereupon he, finding it impossible to make any progress toward an understanding where he could not even get a reply, at last gave up the attempt and became as silent as she.

To poor Annie it was a terrible thought that she should thus have come between mother and son; but she remembered that she had read of mothers who without cause had even hated their own flesh, and how much the more might not she who knew her ambitions and designs so utterly opposed to the desires of her son?

And thereupon all at once awoke in Annie the motherhood that lies deepest of all in the heart of every good woman, making her know in herself that, his mother having forsaken him, she had no choice but take him up and be to him henceforward both wife and mother. What remains of my story will perhaps serve to show how far she succeeded in fulfilling this her vow.

At last Mr. Macintosh saw that things could not thus continue, and that he had better accept an offer made him some time before by a London correspondent—to take Hector into his banking-house and give him the opportunity of widening his experience and knowledge of business; and Hector, on his part, was eager to accept the proposal. The salary offered for his services was certainly not a very liberal one, but the chief attraction was that the hours were even shorter than they had been with his father, and would yet enlarge his liberty of an evening. Hector's delights, as we have seen, had always lain in literature, and in that direction the labor in him naturally sought an outlet. Now there seemed a promise of his being able to pursue it yet more devotedly than before: who could tell but he might ere long produce something that people might care to read? Some publisher might even care to put it in print, and people might care to buy it! That would start him in a more genuine way of living, and he might the sooner be able to marry Annie—an aspiration surely legitimate and not too ambitious. He had had a good education, and considered himself to be ably equipped. It was true he had not been to either Oxford or Cambridge, but he had enjoyed the advantages possessed by a Scotch university even over an English one, consisting mainly in the freedom of an unhampered development. Since then he had read largely, and had cultivated naturally wide sympathies. As his vehicle for utterance, we have already seen that he had a great attraction to verse, and had long held and argued that the best training for effective prose was exercise in the fetters of verse—a conviction in which he had lived long enough to confirm himself, and perhaps one or two besides.

His relations with his mother, and consequent impediments to seeing Annie, took away the sting of having to part with her for a while; and, when he finally closed with the offer, she at once resumed her application for a place in the High School, and was soon accepted, for there were not a few in the town capable of doing justice to her fitness for the office ; so that now she had the joy not merely of being able to live with her mother as before, and of contributing to her income, but of knowing at the same time that she lived in a like atmosphere with Hector, where her growth in the knowledge of literature, and her experience in the world of thought, would be gradually fitting her for a companion to him whom she continued to regard as so much above her. Her marked receptivity in the matter of verse, and her intrinsic discrimination of nature and character in it, became in her, at length, as they grew, sustaining forces, enlarging her powers both of sympathy and judgment, so that soon she came to feel, in reading certain of the best writers, as if she and Hector were looking over the same book together, reading and pondering it as one, simultaneously seeing what the writer meant and felt and would have them see and feel. So that, by the new intervention of space, they were in no sense or degree separated, but rather brought by it actually, that is, spiritually, nearer to each other. Also Hector wrote to her regularly on a certain day of every week, and very rarely disappointed her of her expected letter, in which he uttered his thoughts and feelings more freely than he had ever been able to do in conversation. This also was a gain to her, for thus she went on to know him better and better, rising rapidly nearer to his level of intellectual development, while already she was more than his equal in the moral development which lies at the root of all capacity for intellectual growth. So Annie grew, as surely—without irreverence I may say—in favor both with God and man; for at the same time she grew constantly in that loveliest of all things— humanity.

Nor was Hector left without similar consolation in his life, although passed apart from Annie. For, not to mention the growing pleasure that he derived from poring over Annie's childlike letters —and here I would beg my reader to note the essential distinction betwixt childish and childlike— full of the keenest perceptions and the happiest phrases, he had soon come to make the acquaintance of a kindred spirit, a man whom, indeed, it took a long time really to know, but who, being from the first attracted to him, was soon running down the inclined plane of acquaintanceship with rapidly increasing velocity toward something far better than mere acquaintance: nor was there any check in their steady approach to a thorough knowledge of each other. He was a slightly older man, with a greater experience of men, and a good deal wider range of interests, as could hardly fail to be the case with a Londoner. But the surprising thing to both of them was that they had so many feelings in common, giving rise to many judgments and preferences also in common; so that Hector had now a companion in whom to find the sympathy necessary to the ripening of his taste in such a delicate pursuit as that of verse; and their proclivities being alike, they ran together like two drops on a pane of glass; whence it came that at length, in the confident expectation of understanding and sympathy, Hector found himself submitting to his friend's judgment the poem he had produced when first grown aware that he was in love with Annie Melville; although such was his sensitiveness in the matter of his own productions that hitherto he had not yet ventured on the experiment with Annie herself.

His new friend read, was delighted; read again, and spoke

FAR ABOVE RUBIES

out his pleasure; and then first Hector knew the power of sympathy to double the consciousness of one's own faculty. He took up again the work he had looked upon as finished, and went over it afresh with wider eyes, keener judgment, and clearer purpose; when the result was that, through the criticisms passed upon it by his friend, and the reflection of the poem afresh in his own questioning mind, he found many things that had to be reconsidered; after which he committed the manuscript, carefully and very legibly re-written, once more to his friend, who, having read it yet again, was more thoroughly pleased with it than before, and proposed to Hector to show it to another friend to whom the ear of a certain publisher lay open. The favorable judgment of this second friend was patiently listened to by the publisher, and his promise given that the manuscript should receive all proper attention.

On this part of my story there is no occasion to linger ; for, strange thing to tell,—strange, I mean, from the unlikelihood of its happening,—the poem found the sympathetic spot in the heart of the publisher, who had happily not delegated the task to his reader, but read it himself ; and he made Hector the liberal offer to undertake all the necessary expenses, giving him a fair share of resulting profits.

Stranger yet, the poem was so far a success that the whole edition, not a large one, was sold, with a result in money necessarily small but far from unsatisfactory to Hector. At the publisher's suggestion, this first volume was soon followed by another; and thus was Hector fairly launched on the uncertain sea of a literary life; happy in this, that he was not entirely dependent on literature for his bodily sustenance, but was in a position otherwise to earn at least his bread and cheese. For some time longer he continued to have no experience of the killing necessity of writing for his daily bread, beneath which so many aspiring spirits sink prematurely exhausted and withered; this was happily postponed, for there are as much Providence and mercy in the orderly arrangement of our trials as in their inevitable arrival.

FAR ABOVE RUBIES

His reception by what is called the public was by no means so remarkable or triumphant as to give his well-wishers any ground for anxiety as to its possible moral effect upon him; but it was a great joy to him that his father was much interested and delighted in the reception of the poem by the Reviews in general. He was so much gratified, indeed, that he immediately wrote to him stating his intention of supplementing his income by half as much more.

This reflected opinion of others wrought also to the mollifying of his mother's feelings toward him; but those with which she regarded Annie they only served to indurate, as the more revealing the girl's unworthiness of him. And although at first she regarded with favor her husband's kind intention toward Hector, she faced entirely round when he showed her a letter he had from his son thanking him for his generosity, and communicating his intention of begging Annie to come to him and be married at once.

Annie was living at home, feeding on Hector's letters, and strengthened by her mother's sympathy. She was teaching regularly at the High School, and adding a little to their common income by giving a few music lessons, as well as employing her needle in a certain kind of embroidery a good deal sought after, in which she excelled. She had heard nothing of his having begun to distinguish himself, neither had yet seen one of the reviews of his book, for no one had taken the trouble to show her any of them.

One day, however, as she stood waiting a moment for something she wanted in the principal bookshop of the town, a little old lady, rather shabbily dressed, came in, whom she heard say to the shopman, in a gentle voice, and with the loveliest smile :

"Have you another copy of this new poem by your townsman, young Macintosh?"

"I am sorry I have not, ma'am," answered the shopman ; "but I can get you one by return of post."

"Do, if you please, and send it me at once. I am very glad to hear it promises to be a great success. I am sure it quite deserves it. I have already read it through twice. You may remember you got me a copy the other day. I cannot help thinking it an altogether remarkable production, especially for so young a man. He is quite young, I believe?"

"Yes, ma'am—to have already published a book. But as to any wonderful success, there is so little sale for poetry nowadays. I believe the one you had yourself, my lady, is the only one we have been asked for."

"Much will depend," said the lady, "on whether it finds a channel of its own soon enough. But get me another copy, anyhow—and as soon as you can, please. I want to send it to my daughter.

FAR ABOVE RUBIES

There is matter between those Quaker-like boards that I have found nowhere else. I want my daughter to have it, and I cannot part with my own copy," concluded the old lady, and with the words she walked out of the shop, leaving Annie bewildered, and with the strange feeling of a surprise, which yet she had been expecting. For what else but such success could come to Hector? Had it not been drawing nearer and nearer all the time? And for a moment she seemed again to stand, a much younger child than now, amid the gusty whirling of the dead leaves about her feet, once more on the point of stooping to pick up what *might* prove a withered leaf, but was in reality a pound-note, the thing which had wrought her so much misery, and was now filling her cup of joy to the very brim. The book the old lady had talked of *could* be no other than Hector's book. No other than Hector *could* have written it. What a treasure there was in the world that she had never seen! How big was it? What was it like? She was sure to know it the moment her eyes fell upon it. But why had he never told her about it? He might have wanted to surprise her, but she was not the least surprised. She had known it all the time! He had never talked about what he was writing, and still less would he talk of what he was going to write. Intentions were not worthy of his beautiful mouth! Perhaps he did not want her to read it yet.

When he did, he would send her a copy. And, oh! when would her mother be able to read it? Was it a very dear book? There could be no thought of their buying it! Between them, she and her mother could not have shillings enough for that. When the right time came, he would send it. Then it would be twice as much hers as if she had bought it for herself.

The next day she met Mr. and Mrs. Macintosh, and the former actually congratulated her on what Hector had done and what people thought of him for it; but the latter only gave a sniff. And the next post brought the book itself, and with it a petition from Hector that she would fix the day to join him in London.

Annie made haste, therefore, to

get ready the dress of white linen in which she meant to be married, and a lady, the sister of Hector's friend, meeting her in London, they were married the next day, and went together to Hector's humble lodgings in a northern suburb.

Hector's new volume, larger somewhat, but made up of smaller poems, did not attract the same amount of attention as the former, and the result gave no encouragement to the publisher to make a third venture. One reason possibly was that the subjects of most of the poems, even the gayest of them, were serious, and another may have been that the common tribe of reviewers, searching like other parasites, discovered in them material for ridicule—which to them meant food, and as such they made use of it. At the same time he was not left without friends; certain of his readers, who saw what he meant and cared to understand it, continued his readers; and his influence on such was slowly growing, while those that admired, feeling the power of his work, held by him the more when the scoffers at him grew insolent. Still, few copies were sold, and Hector found it well that he had other work and was not altogether dependent on his pen, which would have been simple starvation. And, from the first, Annie was most careful in her expenditure.

Among the simple people whom her husband brought her to know, she speedily became a great favorite, and this circle widened more rapidly after she joined it. For her simple truth, which even to Hector had occasionally seemed somewhat overdriven, now revealed itself as the ground of her growing popularity. She welcomed all, was faithful to all, and sympathetic with all. Nor was it long before her husband began to study her in order to understand her—and that the more that he could find in her neither plan nor system, nothing but straightforward, foldless simplicity. Nor did she ever come to believe less in the foreseeing care of God. She ceased perhaps to attribute so much to the ministry of the angels as when she took the fiercer blast that rescued from the flames the greasy note and blew it uncharred up the roaring chimney for the sudden waft of an angel's wing; but she came to meet them oftener in daily life, clothed in human form, though still they were rare indeed, and often, like the angel that revealed himself to Manoah, disappeared upon recognition.

By-and-by it seemed certain that, if ever Hector had had anything of what the world counts success, it had now come to a pause. For a long time he wrote nothing that, had it been published, could have produced any impression like that of his first book; it seemed as if the first had forestalled the success of those that should follow. That had been of a new sort, and the so-called Public, innocent little personification, was not yet grown ready for anything more of a similar kind, which, indeed, seemed to lack elements of attraction and interest; and the readers to whom the same man will tell even new things are apt to grow weary of his mode of saying, even though that mode have improved in directness and force; the tide of his small repute had already begun to take the other direction. Those who understood and prized his work, still holding by him, and declaring that they found in him what they found in no other writer, remained stanch in their friendship, and among them the little old lady who had at once welcomed his first poem to her heart and whose name and position were now well known to

Hector. But the reviewers, seeming to have forgotten their first favorable reception of him, now began to find nothing but faults in his work, pointing out only what they judged ill contrived and worse executed in his conceptions, and that in a tone to convey the impression that he had somehow wheedled certain of them into their former friendly utterances concerning him.

And about the same time it so happened that business began to fall away rapidly from the bank of which his father held the chief country agency, so that he was no longer able to continue to Hector his former subsidy, the announcement of which discouraging fact was accompanied by a lecture on the desirableness of a change in his choice of subject as well as in his style; if he continued to write as he had been doing of late, no one would be left, his father said, to read what he wrote!

And now it began to be evident what a happy thing it was for Hector that Annie was now at his side to help him. For, as his courage sank, and he saw Annie began to feel straitened in her housekeeping, he saw also how her courage arose and shone. But he grew more and more discouraged, until it was all that Annie could do to hold him back from despair. At length, however, she began to feel that possibly there might be some truth in what his father had written to him, and a new departure ought to be attempted. She could not herself believe that her husband was limited to any style or subject for the embodiment of his thoughts; he who had written so well in one fashion might write at least well, if not as well, in another! Had she not heard him say that verse was the best practice for writing prose?

Gently, therefore, and cautiously she approached the matter with him, only to find at first, as she had expected, that he but recoiled from the suggestion with increase of discouragement. Still, taking no delight in obstinacy, and feeling the necessity of some fresh attempt grow daily more pressing, he turned his brains about, and sending them foraging, at length bethought him of a certain old Highland legend with which at one time he had been a good deal taken, from the discovery in it of certain symbolical possibilities. This legend he proceeded to rewrite and remodel, doing his best endeavor to preserve in it the old Celtic aroma and aërial suggestion, while taking care neither to lose nor reproduce too manifestly its half-apparent, still evanishing symbolism. Urged by fear and enfeebled by doubt, he wrote feverously, and, after three days of laborious and unnatural toil, submitted the result to Annie, who was now his only representative of the outer world, and the only person for whose criticism he seemed now to care. She, greatly in doubt of her own judgment, submitted it to his friend; and together they agreed on this verdict: That, while it certainly proved he could write as well in prose as in verse, people would not be attracted by it, and that it would be found lacking in human interest. His friend saw in it also too much of the Celtic tendency to the mystical and allegorical, as distinguished from the factual and storial.

Upon learning this their decision, poor Hector fell once more into a state of great discouragement, not feeling in him the least power of adopting another way; there seemed to him but one mode, the way things came to him. And in this surely he was right— only might not things come, or be sent to him in some other way? His friend suggested that he might, changing the outward occurrences, and the description of the persons to whom they happened, in such fashion that there could be no identification of them, tell the very tale of how Annie and he came to know and love each other, taking especial care to muffle up to shapelessness, or at least featurelessness, the part his mother had taken in their story. This seeming to Hector a thing possible, he took courage, and set about it at once, gathering interest as he proceeded, and writing faster and faster as he grew in hope of success. At the same time it was not favorable to the result that he felt constantly behind him, the darkly lowering necessity that, urging him on, yet debilitated every motion of the generating spirit.

FAR ABOVE RUBIES

It took him a long time to get the story into a condition that he dared to consider even passable; and the longer that he had not the delight that verse would have brought with it in the process of its production. Nevertheless he would now and then come to a passage in writing which the old emotion would seem to revive; but in reading these, Annie, modest and doubtful as she always was of her own judgment, especially where her husband's work was concerned, seemed to recognize a certain element of excitement that gave it a glow, or rather, glamour of unreality, or rather, unnaturalness, which affected her as inharmonious, therefore unfit, or out of place. She thought it better, however, to say little or nothing of any such paragraph, and tried to regard it as of small significance, and probably carrying little influence in respect of the final judgment.

The narrative, such as it might prove, was at length finished, and had been read, at least with pleasure and hope, by his friend, who was still the only critic on whose judgment he dared depend, for he could not help regarding Annie as prejudiced in his favor, although her approval continued for him absolutely essential. The sole portions to which his friend took any exception were the same concerning which Annie had already doubted, and which he found too poetical in their tone—not, he took care to say, in their meaning, for that could not be too poetical, but in their expression, which must impinge too sharply upon prosaic ears that cared only for the narrative, and would recoil from any reflection, however just in itself, that might be woven into it.

But, alas, now came what Hector felt the last and final blow to the possibility of farther endeavor in the way of literature!

The bank to which Hector had been introduced by his father, and in which he had been employed ever since, had of late found it necessary to look more closely to its outlay and reduce its expenses; therefore, believing that Hector had abundance of other resources, its managers decided on giving him notice first of all that they must in future deprive themselves of the pleasure of his services. And this announcement came at a time when Annie was already in no small difficulty to make the ends of her expenditure meet those of her income. In fact, she had no longer any income. For a considerable time she had, by the stinting of what had before that seemed necessities, been making a shilling do the work of eighteenpence, and now she knew nothing beyond, except to go without. But how allow Hector to go without? He must die if she did! Already he had begun to shrink in his clothes from lack of proper nourishment.

A rumor reaching him of a certain post as librarian, in the gift of an old corporation, being vacant, Hector at once made application for it, but only to receive the answer that Pegasus must not be put in harness: poor Pegasus, on a false pretense of respect, must be kept out of the shafts! His fat friends would not permit him to degrade himself earning his bread by work he could have done very well; he must rather starve! He tried for many posts, one after the other. Heavier and heavier fell upon him each following disappointment.

Annie had in her heart been greatly disappointed that no prospect appeared of a child to sanctify their union; but for that she had learned more than to console herself with the reflection that at least there was no such heavenly visitor for whose earthly sojourn to provide; and now how gladly would she have labored for the child in the hope that such a joy and companionship might lift him up out of his despondency! Then he would be able to enjoy and assimilate the poor food she was able to get for him. It is true he always seemed quite content; but, then, he would often, she believed, pretend not to be hungry, and certainly ate less and less. Hitherto she had fought with all her might against running in debt to the tradespeople, for, more than all else, she feared debt. Now, at last, however, her resolution was in danger of giving way, when, happily, Hector bethought himself of his precious books; to what better use could he put them than sell them to buy food—wherein the books he had written had failed him? Parcel by parcel in a leather strap, he carried them to the nearest secondhand bookseller, where he had so often bought; now he wanted to sell, but, unhappily, he soon found that books, like many other things, are worth much less to the seller than to the buyer, and where Hector had calculated on pounds, only shillings were forthcoming. Yet by their sale, notwithstanding, they managed to keep a little longer out of debt.

And in these days Annie had at length finished her fair copy of Hector's last book, writing it out in her own lovelily legible hand—not such as ladies in general count legible, because they can easily read it themselves; she could do better than that, she could write so that others could not fail to read. For Hector had always believed that the acceptance of his first volume had been owing not a little to the fact that he had written it out most legibly, and he held that what reveals itself at once and without possibility of mistake may justly hope for a better reception than what from the first moment annoys the reader with a sense of ill-treatment. It is no wonder, he said, if such a manuscript be at once tossed aside with an imprecation. Legibility is the first and intelligibility the only other thing rendered due by the submission of a manuscript to any publisher.

Hector spent a day or two in remodeling and modifying the passages remarked upon by his wife and his friend, and then, with hope reviving in both their hearts, the manuscript was sent in, acknowledged, and the day appointed when an answer would be ready.

Upon a certain dark morning, therefore, in November, having nothing else whatever to do, Hector set out in his much-worn Inverness cape to call upon his former publisher in the City, with whom of late he had had no communication. The weather was cold and damp, threatening rain. But Hector was too much of a Scotchman to care about weather, and too full of anxiety to mind either cold or wet. He had, indeed, almost always felt gloomy weather exciting rather than depressing. For one thing, it seemed, when he was indoors, to close him about with protection from uncongenial interruption, leaving the freer his inventive faculty; and now that he was abroad in it, and no inventive faculty left awake, it seemed to clothe him with congenial sympathy, for the weather was just the same inside him. And now, as he strode along with his eyes on the ground, he scarcely saw any of the objects about him, but sought only the heart of the City, where he hoped to find the publisher in his office, ready to print his manuscript, and advance him a small sum in anticipation of possible profit. So absorbed was he in thought undefined, and so sunk in anxiety as to the answer he was about to receive, that more than once he was nearly run over by the cart of some reckless tradesman—seeming to him, in its overtaking suddenness, the type of prophetic fate already at his heels.

At length, however, he arrived safe in the outer shop, where the books of the firm were exposed to sight, in process of being subscribed for by the trade. There a pert young man asked him to take a seat, while he carried his name to the publisher, and there for some time he waited, reading titles he found himself unable to lay hold of; and there, while he waited, the threatened rain began, and, ere he was admitted to the inner premises, such a black deluge came pouring down as, for blackness at least, comes down nowhere save in London. With this accompaniment, he was ushered at length into a dingy office, deep in the recesses of the house, where a young man whom he saw for the first time had evidently, while Hector waited in the shop, been glancing at the manuscript he had left. Little as he could have read, however, it had been enough, aided perhaps by the weather, to bring him to an unfavorable decision; his rejection was precise and definite, leaving no room for Hector to say anything, for he did not seem ever to have heard of him before. Hector rose at once, gathered up his papers from the table where they lay scattered, said "Good-morning," and went out into the sooty rain.

Not knowing whitherward to point his foot, he stopped at the corner of King William Street, close to the money-shops of the old Lombards, and there stood still, in vain endeavor to realize the blow that had stunned him. There he stood and stood, with bowed head, like an outcast beggar, watching the rain that dropped black from the rim of his saturated hat. Becoming suddenly conscious, however, that the few wayfarers glanced somewhat curiously at him as they passed, he started to walk on, not knowing whither, but trying to look as if he had a purpose somewhere inside him, whereas he had still a question to settle—whether to buy a bun, and, on the strength of that, walk home, or spend his few remaining pence on an omnibus, as far as it would take him for the money, and walk the rest of the way.

Then, suddenly, as if out of the depths of despair, arose in him an assurance of help on the way to him, and with it a strength to look in the face the worst that could befall him; he might at least starve in patience. Therewith he drew himself up, crossed the street to the corner of the Mansion House, and got into an omnibus waiting there.

If only he could creep into his grave and have done! Why should that hostelry of refuge stand always shut? Surely he was but walking in his own funeral! Were not the mourners already going about the street before ever the silver cord was loosed or the golden bowl broken? Might he not now at length feel at liberty to end the life he had ceased to value? But there was Annie! He would go home to her; she would comfort him—yes, she would die with him! There was no other escape; there was no sign of coming deliverance. All was black within and around them. That was the rain on the gravestones. He was in a hearse, on his way to the churchyard. There the mourners were already gathered. They were before him, waiting his arrival. No! He would go home to Annie! He would not be a coward soldier! He would not kill himself to escape the enemy! He would stand up to the Evil One, and take his blows without flinching. He and his Annie would take them together, and fight to the last. Then, if they must die, it was well, and would be better.

But alas! what if the obligation of a live soul went farther than this life? What if a man was bound, by the fact that he lived, to live on, and do everything possible to keep the life alive in him? There his heart sank, and the depths of the sea covered it! Did God require of him that, sooner than die, he should beg the food to keep him alive? Would he be guilty of forsaking his post, if he but refused to ask, and waited for Death? Was he bound to beg? If he was, he must begin at once by refusing to accept the smallest credit! To all they must tell the truth of their circumstances, and refuse aught but charity. But was there not something yet he could try before begging? He had had a good education, had both knowledge and the power of imparting it; this was still worth money in the world's market. And doubtless therein his friend could do something for him.

Therewithal his new dread was gone; one possibility was yet left him in store! To his wife he must go, and talk the thing over with her. He had still, he believed, threepence in his pocket to pay for the omnibus.

It began to move; and then first, waking up, he saw that he had seated himself between a poor woman and a little girl, evidently her daughter.

"I am very sorry to incommode you, ma'am," he said apologetically to the white-faced woman, whose little tartan shawl scarcely covered her shoulders, painfully conscious of his dripping condition, as he took off his hat, and laid it on the floor between his equally soaking feet. But, instead of moving away from him to a drier position beyond, the woman, with a feeble smile, moved closer up to him, saying to her daughter on his other side:

"Sit closer to the gentleman, Jessie, and help to keep him warm. She's quite clean, sir," she added. "We have plenty of water in our place, and I gave her a bath myself this morning, because we were going to the hospital to see my husband. He had a bad accident yesterday, but thank God! not so bad as it might have been.

I'm afraid you're feeling very cold, sir," she added, for Hector had just given an involuntary shiver.

" My husband he's a bricklayer," she went on ; " he has been in good work, and I have a few shillings in hand, thank God ! Times are sure to mend, for they seldom turns out so bad as they looks."

Involuntarily Hector's hand moved to his trouser-pocket, but dropped by his side as he remembered the fare.

She saw his movement, and broke into a sad little laugh.

"Don't mistake me, sir," she resumed. "I told you true when I said I wasn't without money ; and, before the pinch comes, wages, I dare say, will show their color again. Besides, our week's rent is paid. And he's in good quarters, poor fellow, though with a bad pain to keep him company, I'm afraid."

"Where do you live?" asked Hector. "But," he went on, "why should I ask? I am as poor as you—poorer, perhaps, for I have no trade to fall back upon. But I have a good wife like you, and I don't doubt she'll think of something."

"Trust to that, sir! A good woman like I'm sure she is 'll be sure to think of many a thing before she'll give in. My husband, he was brought up to religion, and he always says there's one as know's and don't forget."

But now the omnibus had reached the spot where Hector must leave it. He got up, fumbling for his threepenny-piece, but failed to find it.

"Don't forget your hat, sir; it'll come all right when it's dry," said the woman, as she handed it to him. But he stood, the conductor waiting, and seemed unable to take it from her: he could not find the little coin!

"There, there, sir!" interposed the woman, as she made haste and handed him three coppers; "I have plenty for both of us, and wish for your sake it was a hundred times as much. Take it, sir," she insisted, while Hector yet hesitated and fumbled; "you won't refuse such a small service from another of God's creatures! I mean it well."

But the conductor, apparently affected with the same generosity, pushed back the woman's hand, saying, "No, no, ma'am, thank you! The gentleman 'll pay me another day."

Hector pulled out an old silver watch, and offered it.

"I cannot be so sure about that," he said. "Better take this: it's of little use to me now."

"I'll be damned if I do!" cried the conductor fiercely, and down he jumped and stood ready to help Hector from the omnibus.

But his kindness was more than Hector could stand; he walked away, unable to thank him.

"I wonder now," muttered the conductor to himself when Hector was gone, "if that was a put-up job between him and the woman? I don't think so. Anyhow, it's no great loss to anybody. I won't put it down; the company 'll have to cover that."

Hector turned down a street that led westward, drying his eyes, and winking hard to make them swallow the tears which sought to hide from him a spectacle that was calling aloud to be seen. For lo! the street-end was filled with the glory of a magnificent rainbow. All across its opening stretched and stood the wide arch of a wonderful rainbow. Hector could not see the sun; he saw only what it was making; and the old story came back to him, how the men of ancient time took the heavenly bow for a promise that there should no more be such a flood as again to destroy the world. And therefore even now the poets called the rainbow the bow of hope.

FAR ABOVE RUBIES

Nor, even in these days of question and unbelief, is it matter of wonder that, at sight of the harmony of blended and mingling, yet always individual, and never confused colors, and notwithstanding his knowledge of optics, and of how the supreme unity of the light was secerned into its decreed chord, the imaginative faith of the troubled poet should so work in him as to lift his head for a moment above the waters of that other flood that threatened to overwhelm his microcosm, and the bow should seem to him a new promise, given to him then and individually, of the faithfulness of an unseen Power of whom he had been assured, by one whom he dared not doubt, that He numbered the very hairs of his head.

FAR ABOVE RUBIES

Once more his spirit rose upon the wave of a hope which he could neither logically justify nor dare to refuse; for hope is hope whencesoever it spring, and needs no justification of its self-existence or of its sudden marvelous birth. The very hope was in itself enough for itself. And now he was near his home; his Annie was waiting for him; and in another instant his misery would be shared and comforted by her! He was walking toward the wonder-sign in the heavens. But even as he walked with it full in view, he saw it gradually fade and dissolve into the sky, until not a thread of its loveliness remained to show where it had spanned the infinite with its promise of good. And yet, was not the sky itself a better thing, and the promise of a yet greater good? He must walk onward yet, in tireless hope! And the resolve itself endured—or fading, revived, and came again, and ever yet again.

For ere he had passed the few yards that lay between him and Annie yet another wonder befell: as if the rainbow had condensed, and taken shape as it melted away, there on the pathway, in the thickening twilight of the swift-descending November night, stood a creature, surely not of the night, but rather of the early morn, a lovely little child—whether wandered from the open door of some neighboring house, or left by the vanished rainbow, how was he to tell? Endeavoring afterward to recall every point of her appearance, he could remember nothing of her feet, or even of the frock she wore. Only her face remained to him, with its cerulean eyes—the eyes of Annie, looking up from under the cloud of her dark hair, which also was Annie's. She looked then as she stood, in his memory of her, as if she were saying, "I trust in you; will you not trust in Him who made the rainbow?" For a moment he seemed to stand regarding her, but even while he looked he must have forgotten that she was there before him, for when again he knew that he saw her, though he did not seem ever to have looked away from her, she had changed in the gathering darkness to the phantasm of a daisy, which still gazed up in his face trustingly, and, indeed, went with him to his own door, seeming all the time to say, "It was no child; it was me you saw, and nothing but me; only I saw the sun—I mean, the man that was making the rainbow." And never more could he in his mind separate the child, whom I cannot but think he had verily seen, from the daisy which certainly he had not seen, except in the atmosphere of his troubled and confused soul.

It may help my reader to understand its confusion if I recall to him the fact that Hector had that day eaten nothing. Nor must my wife reader think hardly of Annie for having let him leave the house without any food, for he had stolen softly away, and closed the door as softly behind him, thinking how merrily they would eat together when he came back with his good news. And now he was bringing nothing to her but the story of a poor woman and her child who had warmed him, and of an omnibus-conductor who had trusted him for his fare, and of a rainbow and a child and a daisy.

"Oh, you naughty, naughty dear!" cried Annie, as she threw herself into his arms, rejoicing. But at sight of his worn and pallid face the smile faded from hers, and she thought, "What can have befallen him?"

His lip quivered, and, seeking with a watery smile to reassure her, he gave way and burst into tears. Unmanly of him, no doubt, but what is a man to do when he cannot help it? And where is a man to weep if not on his wife's bosom? Call this behavior un-English, if you will; for, indeed, Hector was in many ways other than English, and, I protest, English ways are not all human. But I will not allow that it manifested any weakness, or necessarily involved shame to him; the best of men, and the strongest—yea, the one Man whose soul harbored not an atom of self-pity—upon one occasion wept, I think because he could not persuade the women whom he loved and would fain console to take comfort in his Father. Annie, for one reverent moment, turned her head aside, then threw her arms about him, and hid her glowing face in his bosom.

"There's only me in the house,

dear," she said, and led the way to their room.

When they reached it, she closed the door, and turned to him.

"So they won't take your story?" she said, assuming the fact, with a sad, sunny smile.

"They refused it absolutely."

"Well, never mind! I shall go out charing to-morrow. You have no notion how strong I am. It is well for you I have never wanted to beat you. Seriously, I believe I am much stronger than you have the least notion of. There! Feel that arm—I should let you feel it another way, only I am afraid of hurting you."

She had turned up the sleeve of her dress, and uncovered a grandly developed arm, white as milk, and blossoming in a large, splendidly formed hand. Then playfully, but oh! so tenderly, with the under and softest part of her arm she fondled his face, rubbing it over first one, then the other cheek, and ended with both arms round his neck, her hands folding his head to her bosom.

"Wife! wife!" faltered Hector, with difficulty controlling himself; "my strong, beautiful wife! To think of your marrying me for this!"

"Hector," answered Annie, drawing herself back with dignity, "do you dare to pity me? That would be to insult me! As if I was not fit to be your wife when doing *everything* for my mother! There are thousands of Scotch girls that would only be proud to take my place, poor as you are—and you couldn't be much poorer—and serve you, without being your wife, as I have the honor and pride to be! But, my blessed man, I do believe you have eaten nothing to-day; and here am I fancying myself your wife, and letting you stand there empty, instead of bestirring myself to get you some supper! What a shame! Why, you are actually dying with hunger!" she cried, searching his face with pitiful eyes.

"On the contrary, I am not in the least hungry," protested Hector.

"Then you must be hungry at once, sir. I will go and bring you something the very sight of which will make you hungry."

"But you have no money, Annie; and, not being able to

pay, we must go without. Come, we will go to bed."

"Yes, I am ready; I had a good breakfast. But you have had nothing all day. And for money, do you know Miss Hamper, the dressmaker, actually offered to lend me a shilling, and I took it. Here it is. You see, I was so sure you would bring money home that I thought we *might* run that much farther into debt. So I got you two fresh eggs and such a lovely little white loaf. Besides, I have just thought of something else we could get a little money for—that dainty chemise my mother made for me with her own hands when we were going to be married. I will take it to the pawnbroker to-morrow."

"I was never in a pawnshop,

Annie. I don't think I should know how to set about it."

"*You!*" cried Annie, with a touch of scorn. "Do you think I would trust a man with it? No; that's a woman's work. Why, you would let the fellow offer you half it was worth—and you would take it too. I shall show it to Mrs. Whitmore: *she* will know what I ought to get for it. She's had to do the thing herself—too often, poor thing!"

"It would be like tearing my heart out."

"What! to part with my pretty chemise. Hector, dear, you must not be foolish! What does it matter, so long as we are not cheating anybody? The pawnshop is a most honorable and useful institution. No one is the worse for it, and many a one the better. Even the tradespeople will be a trifle the better. I shall be quite proud to know that I have a pawn-ticket in my pocket to fall back upon. Oh, there's that old silk dress your mother sent me—I do believe that would bring more. It is in good condition, and looks quite respectable. If Eve had got into a scrape like ours, she would have been helpless, poor thing, not having anything *to put away*—that is the right word, I believe. There is really nothing disgraceful about it. Come now, dear, and eat your eggs—I'm afraid you must do without butter. I always preferred a piece of dry bread with an egg—you get the true taste of the egg so much better. One day or another we must part with everything. It is sure to come. Sooner or later, what does that matter? 'The readiness is all,' as Hamlet says. Death, or the pawnshop, signifies nothing. 'Since no man has aught of what he leaves, what is it to leave betimes?' We do but forestall the grave for one brief hour with the pawnshop."

"You deserve to have married Epictetus, Annie, you brave woman, instead of Xantippe!"

"I prefer you, Hector."

"But what might you have said if he had asked you, and you had heard me bemoaning the pawnshop?"

"Ah, then, indeed! But, in the meantime, we will go to bed and wait there for to-morrow. Is it not a lovely thing to know that God is thinking about you? He will bring us to *our desired haven*, Hector, dearest!"

So in their sadness they laid them down. Annie opened her arms and took Hector to her bosom. There he sighed himself to sleep; and God put His arms about them both, and kept them asleep until the morning.

And in this love, more than in bed, I rest.

Annie was the first to spring up and begin to dress herself, pondering in her mind as she did so whether to go first to the pawnbroker's or to the baker, to ask him to recommend her as a charwoman. She would tell him just the truth—that she must in future work for her daily bread. Then Hector rose and dressed himself.

"Oh, Annie!" he said, as he did so, "is it gone, that awful misery of last night in the omnibus? It seemed, as I jolted along, as if God had forgotten one of the creatures he had made, and that one was me; or, worse, that he thought of me, and would not move to help me! And why do I feel now as if He had help for me somewhere near waiting for me? I think I will go and see a man who lives somewhere close by, and find out if he is the same I used to know at St. Andrews; if he be the same, he may know of something I could try for."

"Do," replied Annie. "I will go with you, and on the way call at the grocer's—I think he will be the best to ask if he knows of any family that wants a charwoman or could give me any sort of work. There's more than one kind of thing I could turn my hand to—needlework, for instance. I could make a child's frock as well, I believe, as a second-rate dressmaker. Can you tell me who was the first tailor, Hector? It was God himself. He made coats of skins for Adam and his wife."

"Quite right, dear. You may well try your hand—as I know you have done many a time already. And, if I can get hold of ever so young a pupil, I shall be glad even to teach him his letters. We must try anything and everything. We are long past being fastidious, I hope."

He turned and went on with his toilet.

"Oh, Hector," said Annie suddenly, and walked to the mantelpiece, "I am so sorry! Here is a letter that came for you yesterday. I did not care to open it, though you have often told me to open any letters I pleased. The fact is, I forgot all about it; I believe, because I was so unhappy at your going away without breakfast. Or perhaps it was that I was frightened at its black border. I really can't tell now why I did not open it."

With little interest and less hope, Hector took the letter,—black-bordered and black-sealed,—opened it, and glanced carelessly at the signature, while Annie stood looking at him, in the hope merely that he would find in it no fresh trouble—some forgotten bill perhaps! She saw his face change, and his eyes grow fixed. A moment more and the letter dropped in the fender. He stood an instant, then fell on his knees, and threw up his hands.

"What is it, darling?" she cried, beginning to tremble.

"Only five hundred pounds!" he answered, and burst into an hysterical laugh.

"Impossible!" cried Annie.

"Who *can* have played us such a cruel trick?" said Hector feebly.

"It's no trick, Hector!" exclaimed Annie. "There's nobody would have the heart to do it. Let *me* see the letter."

She almost caught it from his

hands as he picked it from the fender, and looked at the signature.

"Hale & Hale?" she read. "I never heard of them!"

"No, nor anyone else, I dare say," answered Hector.

"Let us see the address at the top," said Annie.

"There it is—Philpot Lane."

"Where is that? I don't believe there is such a place!"

"Oh, yes, there is; I've seen it—somewhere in the City, I believe. But let us read the letter. I saw only the figures. I confess I was foolish enough at first to fancy semebody had sent us five hundred pounds!"

"And why not?" cried Annie. "I am sure there's no one more in want of it."

"That's just why not," answered

Hector. "Did you ever know a rich man leave his money to a poor relation? Oh, I hope it does not mean that my father is gone. He may have left us a trifle. Only he could not have had so much to leave to anybody. I know he loved you, Annie."

In the meantime Annie had been doing the one sensible thing —reading the letter, and now she stood pondering it.

"I have it, Hector. He always uses good people to do his kindnesses. Don't you remember me telling you about the little old lady in Graham's shop the time your book came out?"

"Yes, Annie; I wasn't likely to forget that; it was my love for you that made me able to write the poem. Ah, but how soon was the twenty pounds I got for it spent, though I thought it riches then!"

"So it was—and so it is!" cried Annie, half laughing, but crying outright. "It's just that same little old lady. She was so delighted with the book, and with you for writing it, that she put you down at once in her will for five hundred pounds, believing it would help people to trust in God."

"And here was I distrusting so much that I was nearly ready to kill myself. Only I thought it would be such a terrible shock to you, my precious! It would have been to tell God to his face that I knew he would not help me. I am sure now that he is never forgetting, though he seems to have forgotten. There was that letter lying in the dark through all the hours of the long night, while we slept in the weariness of sorrow and fear, not knowing what the light was bringing us. God is good!"

"Let us go and see these people and make sure," said Annie. "'Hale and Hearty,' do they call themselves? But I'm going with you myself this time! I'm not going to have such another day as I had yesterday—waiting for you till the sun was down, and all was dark, you bad man!—and fancying all manner of terrible things! I wonder—I wonder, if——"

"Well, what do you wonder, Annie?"

"Only whether, if now we were to find out it was indeed all a mistake, I should yet be able to hope on through all the rest. I doubt it; I doubt it! Oh, Hector, you have taught me everything!"

"More, it seems, than I have myself learned. Your mother had already taught you far more than ever I had to give you!"

"But it is much too early yet, I fear, to call in the City," said Annie. "Don't you think we should have time first to find out whether the gentleman we were thinking of inquiring after to-day be your old college friend or not? And I will call at the grocer's, and tell him we hope to settle his bill in a few days. Then you can come to me, and I will go to you, and we shall meet somewhere between."

They did as Annie proposed;

and before they met, Hector had found his friend, and been heartily received both by him and by his young wife.

When at length they reached Philpot Lane, and were seated in an outer room waiting for admission, Annie said: "Surely, if rich people knew how some they do not know need their help, they would be a little more eager to feather their wings ere they fly aloft by making friends with the Mammon of unrighteousness. Don't you think it may be sometimes that they are afraid of doing harm with their money?"

"I'm afraid it is more that they never think what our Lord meant when he said the words. But oh, Annie! is it a bad sign of me that the very possibility of this money could make me so happy?"

They were admitted at length, and kindly received by a gray-haired old man, who warned them not to fancy so much money would last them very long.

"Indeed, sir," answered Annie, "the best thing we expect from it is that it will put my husband in good heart to begin another book."

"Oh! your husband writes books, does he? Then I begin to understand my late client's will. It is just like her," said the old gentleman. "Had you known her long?"

"I never once saw her," said Hector.

"But I did," said Annie, "and I heard her say how delighted she was with his first book. Please, sir," she added, "will it be long before you can let us have the money?"

"You shall have it by-and-by," answered the lawyer; "all in good time."

And now first they learned that not a penny of the money would they receive before the end of a twelvemonth.

"Well, that will give us plenty of time to die first," thought Hector, "which I am sure the kind lady did not intend when she left us the money."

Another thing they learned was that, even then, they would not receive the whole of the money left them, for seeing they could claim no relation to the legator, ten per cent. must be deducted from their legacy. If they came to him in a year from the date of her death, he told them he would have much pleasure in handing them the sum of four hundred and fifty pounds.

So they left the office—not very exultant, for they were both rather hungry, and had to go at once in search of work—with but a poor chance of borrowing upon it.

Nevertheless, Hector broke the silence by saying:

"I declare, Annie, I feel so light and free already that I could invent anything, even a fairy tale, and I feel as if it would be a lovely one. I hope you have a penny left to buy a new bottle of ink. The ink at home is so thick it takes three strokes to one mark."

"Yes, dear, I have a penny; I have two, indeed—just twopence left. We shall buy a bottle of ink with one, and—shall it be a bun with the other? I think one penny bun will divide better than two halfpenny ones."

"Very well. Only, mind, *I'm* to divide it. But, do you know, I've been thinking," said Hector, "whether we might not take a holiday on the strength of our expectations, for we shall have so long to wait for the money that I think we may truly say we have *great* expectations."

"I think we should do better," answered Annie, "to go back to your old friend, Mr. Gillespie, and tell him of our good-fortune, and see whether he can suggest anything for us to do in the meantime."

FAR ABOVE RUBIES

Hector agreed, and together they sought the terrace where Mr. and Mrs. Gillespie lived, who were much interested in their story; and then first they learned that the lady was at least well enough off to be able to help them, and, when they left, she would have Annie take with her a dozen of her handkerchiefs, to embroider with her initials and crest; but Annie begged to be allowed to take only one, that Mrs. Gillespie might first see how she liked her work.

"For, then, you see," she said to her husband, as they went home, "I shall be able to take it back to her this very evening and ask her for the half-crown she offered me for doing it, which I should not have had the face to do with eleven more of them still in my possession. I have no doubt of her being satisfied with my work; and in a week I shall have finished the half of them, and we shall be getting on swimmingly."

Throughout the winter Hector wrote steadily every night, and every night Annie sat by his side and embroidered—though her embroidery was not *all* for other people. Many a time in after years did their thoughts go back to that period as the type of the happy life they were having together.

The next time Hector went to see Mr. Gillespie, that gentleman suggested that he should give a course of lectures to ladies upon English Poetry, beginning with the Anglo-Saxon poets, of whom

Gillespie said he knew nothing, but would be glad to learn a great deal. He knew also, he said, some ladies in the neighborhood willing to pay a guinea each for a course of, say, half-a-dozen such lectures. They would not cost Hector much time to prepare, and would at once bring in a little money. Coleridge himself, he suggested, had done that kind of thing.

"Yes," said Hector, "but he was Coleridge. I have nothing to say worth saying."

"Leave your hearers to judge of that," returned Gillespie. "Do your best, and take your chance. I promise you two pupils at least not over-critical—my wife and myself. It is amazing how little those even who imagine they love it know about English poetry."

"But where should I find a room?" Hector still objected.

"Would not this drawing room do?" asked his friend.

"Splendidly!" answered Hector. "But what will Mrs. Gillespie say to it?"

"She and I are generally of one mind—about people, at least."

"Then I will go home at once and set about finding what to say."

"And I will go out at once and begin hunting you up an audience."

Gillespie succeeded even better than he had anticipated; and there was at the first lecture a very fair gathering indeed. When it was over, the one that knew most of the subject was the young lecturer's wife.

FAR ABOVE RUBIES

The first course was followed by two more, the third at the request of almost all his hearers. And the result was that, before the legacy fell due, Annie had paid all their debts and had not contracted a single new one.

But when the happy day dawned Annie was not able to go with her husband to receive the money; neither did Hector wish that she had been able, for he was glad to go alone. By her side lay a lovely woman-child peacefully asleep. Hector declared her the very image of the child the rainbow left behind as it vanished.

One day, when the mother was a little stronger, she called Hector to her bedside, and playfully claimed the right to be the child's godmother, and to give it her name.

"And who else can have so good a right?" answered Hector. Yet he wondered just a little that Annie should want the child named after herself, and not after her mother.

But when the time for the child's baptism came, Annie, who would hold the little one herself, whispered in the ear of the clergyman:

"The child's name is Iris."

I have told my little story. But perhaps my readers will have patience with me while I add just one little inch to the tail of the mouse my mountain has borne.

Hector's next book, although never so popular as in any outward sense to be called a success, yet was not quite a failure even in regard to the money it brought him, and even at the present day has not ceased to bring in something. Doubtless it has faults not a few, but, happily, the man who knows them best is he who wrote it, and he has never had to repent that he did write it. And now he has an audience on which he can depend to welcome whatever he writes. That he has enemies as well goes without saying, but they are rather scorners than revilers, and they have not yet caused him to retaliate once by criticising any work of theirs. Neither, I believe, has he ever failed to recognize what of genuine and good work most of them have produced. One of the best results to himself of his constant endeavor to avoid jealousy is that he is still able to write verse, and continues to take more pleasure in it than in telling his tales. And still his own test of the success of any of his books is the degree to which he enjoyed it himself while writing it.

His legacy has long been spent, and he has often been in straits since; but he has always gathered good from those straits, and has never again felt as if slow walls were closing in upon him to crush him. And he has hopes by God's help, and with Annie's, of getting through at last, without ever having dishonored his high calling.

The last time I saw him, he introduced his wife to me—having just been telling me his and her story—with the rather enigmatical words:

FAR ABOVE RUBIES

"This is my wife. You cannot see her very well, for, like Hamlet, I wear her 'in my heart's core, aye, in my heart of hearts!'"

THE END.

www.ingramcontent.com/pod-product-compliance
Lightning Source LLC
Chambersburg PA
CBHW020249170426
43202CB00008B/296